MARIE ANTOINETTE

The last Queen of France

THE HISTORY HOUR

HISTORY

CONTENTS

❧ I ❧

INTRODUCTION

❦

As you begin to read this book, you will undoubtedly feel that Queen Marie Antoinette and King Louise XVI led spoiled lives. You will be right in what you think; but you will also find out that with their parents arranging their marriages at a very young age, neither of them was ever able to experience the feelings of young love.

❦

Because Antoinette was from Austria, she had to be married twice, once in Austria and then again in France. When married in Austria her husband to be could not be present, so, weird as it seemed, her brother stood in for the groom.

❦

To travel to France at that time in our history took twenty-three days by carriage so I cannot imagine how dirty and tired they all felt before they had made it to King Louis XVI's castle and immediately upon Antoinette's arrival it was time for the wedding. She must have been exhausted.

❧

You will find that she nor her husband had anything in common and were totally unsuited for each other. They respected each other, but that never takes the place of true love.

❧

As you read further, you will see what horrors and terrors that Louis XVI, Marie Antoinette, their children, and Louis' sister had to suffer through for four years before their deaths. If you could just put yourself in their shoes, it will bring tears to your eyes.

❧

You will realize that they in no way deserved the treatment they received and then you will read how they were forced to meet their deaths.

❧

Before you complete reading this book, you should have gained a bit of admiration for both of them. It is a pity for one to die so young.

❧ II ❦

THE ARRIVAL OF A DOOMED FUTURE QUEEN

"There is nothing new except what has been forgotten."

— MARIE ANTOINETTE

❧❦

November 2nd, 1755 which was a Sunday, after being in labor all day long, Empress Maria Theresa and Emperor Francis Stephen, her husband welcomed into the world their eleventh and last daughter and their fifteenth child.

❧❦

She was born that evening in an armchair somewhere in a room at the Hofburg Palace located in Vienna, Austria.

⚜

The day before her birth at 9:40 a.m., there had been a tremendous earthquake in the city of Lisbon, Portugal over 2,000 miles away that registered at a 9.0-10.0 on the Richter scale. It was followed by a tsunami wave of ten feet high in some places and twenty feet in other areas along with a sequence of fires which devastated the entire city.

⚜

In all the flames and collapsed ruins, it was estimated that 100,000 people died. Countless homes were destroyed or lay in ruins, and this included all essential palaces, churches and royal buildings that belonged to the Court of Portugal. It could be felt thousands of miles away from the epicenter.

⚜

A newspaper published in Portugal at the time, described it on November 1, 1755, as it will always be remembered through the centuries due to the fires and earthquake that has destroyed most of the city of Lisbon. It is fortunate that the safes of Royal Exchequer, and those of several private citizens, were recovered from the ruins.

⚜

The earthquake felt from far away hadn't stopped the birth, and out of reverence to the Virgin Mary, all of the Habsburg princesses became christened as Maria and this new arrival which was baptized November 3rd, 1755, was given the name Maria Antonia Josepha Joanna, but the family called her Antoine (until she moved to France). Her day of baptism was also called 'the Feast of the Dead in the Catholic Austrian calendar.

As soon as she was born, her mother gave her to a wet nurse, and during her first winter, she lived in the nursery wing of the palace. Her mother, Empress Maria Theresa, had a hectic routine every day. In the summer it began at 4:00 a.m., and in the winter it started at 6:00 a.m. The Empress was much too busy and absorbed in handling the affairs of Vienna to take time for her children.

During the summer, the entire family would go to the Schonbrunn Palace out in the countryside where they could walk among the gardens and play in the parkland and woods and all fifteen children were able to run wild.

The first official appearance of Antoine was at her father's birthday party in 1759, when she was only three years old. While some of her sisters and brothers played music to accompany her, Antoine sang a French song.

They were quite a musical family, and young Mozart came to Hofburg in 1762 by invitation. There is a story that Mozart at six years old slipped and fell on their polished floor when Antoine, also six years old, came running to help him and kissed him. Mozart turned to Antoine and told her she was kind and that he would like to marry her. It gave everyone present a good laugh.

❧

Antoine was lucky as she had a pretty carefree childhood and very little education. What education she had was like that of any other 18th-century girl of the aristocracy, and it focused mainly on moral standards and religion. Her brothers, on the other hand, studied extra on academic subject matter.

❧

When Antoine was nine years old, in 1765, Louis Ferdinand was also known as Louis, Dauphin de France, who was the son of the French monarch, Louis XV, expired. When he died, it left the King's eleven-year-old grandson, Louis Auguste, as the heir to France's throne. It was mere months when Marie Antoinette and the grandson, now the future King Louis XVI, became pledged by their parents to marry each other.

❧

Antonia received a new governess to make sure that she would speak French fluently and as her first language instead of German. Antonia's teeth were very crooked, so it was necessary to have a dentist to come in and straighten them. Then a professional hair stylist was brought in to style her hair perfectly and give her a new look. Her portrait was then made and sent off to France.

❧

Realizing how uneducated Antoine was, the King of France in 1768, sent a tutor to work with the future wife of his grandson and teach her the important things she needed to be educated on to be regarded a good queen.

✿

When the tutor returned after spending time with Marie Antoinette, he told the king that she was smarter than what he thought she would be, but she is kind of lazy and wants to party all the time, making it hard to teach her. One must consider that Antoinette was only fourteen years old, with blue-gray eyes, ash-blonde hair, and was so delicately beautiful.

ANTOINETTE'S FUTURE
HUSBAND IS BORN

❦

Louis was born in the early hours at 6:24 a.m. on the ground floor at the Palace of Versailles in 1755. His mother had only labored three hours before he made his entrance into the world. A popular obstetrician had been called to be there, and they had sent a message to the new baby's grandfather, King Louis XV.

❦

A royal birth required many witnesses with the Keeper of the Seals and the Chancellor being present was a must. They promptly baptized the new baby boy as Louis Auguste per the Royal cleric on duty. The King came in quickly to visit his latest grandchild and daughter-in-law, on whom he doted.

❦

There was not a big fuss made as they had no reason to think that Louis-Auguste would ever have the chance to be a king. Think about it; he was the third son of Dauphin Louis-Ferdinand and Marie-Josephe of Saxony. Their eldest boy, the Duc de Bourgogne, was only three. The second son, the Duc d'Aquitaine, they would soon learn, would die before his first birthday.

⚜

There would be two younger brothers that would be coming along quickly: The Comte de Provence (later Louis XVIII) and Comte D'Artois (Charles X).

⚜

The Dauphin was a very religious man and therefore gave his new baby boy the name of Louis-Auguste in honor of his sainted King Louis XII. The little guy growing up was told over and over to emulate his godly relative.

⚜

The new baby boy ran into trouble at the start of his life. His wet nurse did not have any milk, but it was almost impossible to have her replaced since she was sleeping with the man in charge of their royal household who, unfortunately, was the only one who had the authority to fire her.

⚜

Louis-Auguste was emaciated, reckless and just stuck out as the odd one of the family. He did not look anything like his brothers. He had a fair complexion, and his blue eyes bulged from his head; both he inherited from his Mum who was a

Saxon. He had hooded eyelids, heavy eyebrows, he was clumsy, and a heaviness about him that you could not disguise.

❁

His brother Bourgogne was bossy and boisterous, Artois had good looks and charm, Provence was the amusing and lively one. Berry was introverted and slow. He was also evasive and timid, and he spent time dancing attendance on the assertive Bourgogne, who was always cheating him whenever they played cards.

❁

It was clear that the Dauphine and Dauphin were very close and during fourteen years of their marriage, she had eleven miscarriages and eight children. The Dauphin believed in a good education and took great pains with his sons, who he made sure they had a full array of tutors that taught them in Latin, physics, geography, dancing, scripture, mathematics, history, and fencing.

❁

The Young Louis-Auguste was educated in metalwork that he dearly loved, and in carpentry which he hated as much as he loved the metalwork. Special plays written for the princes were put on for them, but they seemed to be so full of bullying that it made Louis-Auguste hate the theatre from then on.

❁

In 1761 at the age of ten Bourgogne died from tuberculosis. Bourgogne was the 'hope' of the entire family to carry on for them, and his mother and father seemed to never recover from his death. It was so difficult for them to imagine Louis-Auguste as the substitute for the King.

⚜

The Dauphin fell ill with tuberculosis and was exceedingly calm while preparing for his death. He took this chance to educate his children that princesses and princes are susceptible to diseases and dying just like everyone else. The Dauphin with his entire family, foreign ambassadors, and the court present was given his last rites of the Church and died toward the end of 1765 when Louis-Auguste was only eleven. Only two years later, Louis-Auguste would write in briefly in his journal:

"Death of mother at eight in the evening."

⚜

It made Louis-Auguste a Dauphin. At the age of fifteen, he would marry the lively Antoinette of Austria, who was the exact opposite of him. He turned nineteen years old before he succeeded his grandpa to the throne in 1774 and he had no idea that half his life was already over.

❧ III ❧
TWO SHALL BECOME
ONE OR NOT?

"My tastes are not those of the king, who has none, except for hunting and mechanic's labour."

— MARIE ANTOINETTE

❦❧

At fourteen years old in May of 1770, Marie Antoinette set out to travel to France from Austria to be married. She was escorted by 376 horses, 117 footmen, and 57 carriages; so, she and Louis Auguste were planning on being married May 16, 1770. The journey to Paris lasted 23 days when they arrived on the very day of the wedding.

❦❧

Few people realize it, but before the main royal wedding in

Paris Antoinette and Louis were what was considered legally married in her country of Austria, but the groom was not there. Antoinette's brother Ferdinand played as her groom that day.

❦

The day Antoinette left for Paris her mother told her to

> *"Do so much good for the people of France that they*
> *will be able to say that I have sent them*
> *an angel."*

As we well know, that did not happen.

❦

Antoinette's dress was designed from silver cloth because the Dauphine's used that as the customary color for brides and it shined so that when you looked at it, it appeared as white. The dress was covered in pearls and diamonds that her mother had gifted to her.

❦

As Marie Antoinette walked down the Hall of Mirrors toward the royal chapel, it is said the diamonds sparkled thousands of times.

❦

Antoinette's dress for her wedding had large panniers, what is called hip pads today. (It looked like a two by four sticking out from either side of her hips with the fabric draped across it.) The 'panniers' made Antoinette's silhouette significantly broader than what it was from her waist down.

⚜

What caused all the gossip about the way Antoinette was showing so much of herself on her wedding day was the bodice of her dress. Antoinette's gown had been designed and sewn before she had arrived in Paris and was made off 'estimates' of what they thought her measurements were at the time.

⚜

She had not tried on the dress until the very day of her wedding, and everyone could tell it was too small.

⚜

The ladies of the court had worked hard on her dress, but nevertheless, they could not lace it up entirely in the back, so Marie Antoinette's slip showed through. The wedding dress was just too small, and it left a wide opening in the back of the dress that could not be fixed because all the fabric was still in Austria. It looked very unprofessional with the slip shining between the broad strips of diamonds down the back. Her dress was dripping in jewels.

⚜

The groom, however, looked scared to death, he was trembling, worn down with anxiety, but dressed in a suit of gold that was also covered with all sorts of jewels.

❧

The bride was smiling and poised and appeared no older than twelve years old; she appeared with her head held high with a heavy silver brocade gown adorned with a heavy, long train. Her tiny figure glittered all over with diamonds and other jewels.

❧

Louis-Auguste de France married Maria Antonia Josepha Johanna von Habsburg-Lothringen on May 16th, 1770. It was an incredibly lavish affair at Versailles. More than 5,000 guests were in attendance and admitted only if they possessed a ticket. There were over 200,000 curious onlookers that came up to the palace to try and see the royal couple. Even those who had not been officially invited. They came even though they had to awaken at 6 a.m. to dress and reach the palace in time to try and catch a glimpse.

❧

All invited guests were required to wear full court dress. It meant for the women that they must wear hooped skirts, long trains, tightly boned bodices and be elaborately dressed with powdered hair while men had to wear silk coats and swords.

❧

When it was time for them to sign the marriage contract, Antoinette signed on the line where she had been instructed to; but she accidentally allowed a huge blot of the ink to fall

on the contract that covered over half her name. It was seen
to be a bad omen which they did not need for their future.

❦

In the palace, the wedding day ended amazingly. The aristo-
crats, in their lavish attire, who wanted to see, but more
importantly, wanted to be seen all crowded into the different
areas of the castle. A splendid supper was served to all in the
theatre where it had been made into a banquet hall, and the
lighting was from an immense number of candles. The ladies
were all dressed so beautifully, making the scene so
magnificent.

❦

The foods served were very rich and different than what
Antoinette usually ate in her homeland. Here in Paris, a
typical meal contained sixteen courses and then multiple
towers of elegant desserts.

❦

As the wedding party ate, all the people in attendance
watched. Louis, her new husband, liked to eat and was a
hearty eater. Antoinette lost her appetite; (in this writer's
opinion it could have been because of the way her husband
ate.)

❦

After the wedding banquet, Antoinette and Louis danced in
front of everyone to the minuet without making one mistake.

The day of the wedding was full of downpours, so the fireworks display had to be delayed. However, the celebrations
carried on for two weeks, and the fireworks display was held
at the Place de la Concorde on May 30th and suddenly took a
tragic turn when the fireworks display started a riot for some
reason, and 132 people were trampled to death. It was the
beginning of a grim omen of their reign that would prove
tragic in so many ways.

That evening after the ceremonies of the wedding that day,
the groom's grandfather escorted his grandson and his new
granddaughter-in-law to their room. The archbishop blessed
the wedding bed. The king then gave the groom his sleeping
shirt. Some of the pessimists that were present felt that the
thunder and the storm that day was another omen from
heaven and when the Antoinette signed the marriage register,
well the marriage was doomed no matter how you looked
at it.

The king gave them both a kiss and left their wedding cham-
ber, so they could start working on giving him an heir to the
throne. Nothing happened that night between the two and
apparently for the next seven years, but not without reason.

It seems her groom had a painful condition that caused him
to be impotent and this caused Palace gossip to spread far

and wide. Some of the chatter included that Antoinette was a lesbian which was never proved. It was felt the new King suffered from phimosis which is congenital and there is a narrowing at the opening in the foreskin of the penis, so it cannot be pulled back or retracted over the head of the penis. It makes sex very painful and cools the urge.

❦

Marie Antoinette did not like married life, and it was evident that she had not been ready to be married; because her letters she wrote back home showed just how intense her homesickness. She started her letters with

"my very dear mother,"

which she wrote in one letter,

"I have not gotten any of your letters without crying when I read them."

❦

She hated some of the things she had to do being a '***lady***' in the French Royal Family. She complained that she had to wash her hands and put on her makeup in front of God and the rest of the world.

❦

Just to get dressed every day took Antoinette hours. To get her hair fixed each day required the hairdresser to put a wire structure on her head that was three-foot-tall or higher and then her hair arranged around the wire, followed by powdering it with flour, then it was decorated with flowers and jewels.

❦

Then her face would be covered with a white paste before the red rouge was applied. She always wore heavy velvet, brocade and silk gowns with lots of lace and tight corsets that were miserable and accented with high heel shoes made of satin.

❦

She not only had access to the French crown jewels but among them was the beautiful "*Hope Diamond*." that was worn by the King. Antoinette loved diamonds and often had them in her hair.

❦

After her husband had his surgery they had four children:

- Marie Therese Charlotte 1778-1851
- Louis Joseph Xavier Francois 1781-1789
- Louis Charles 1785-1795
- Sophie Beatrix 1786-1786

❦

It was during the birth process of Antoinette's first baby on December 9, 1778, which was a girl that she named Marie Therese Charlotte after Antoinette's mother when Antoinette went into a seizure and collapsed. Being in labor for twelve hours after all in a very stuffy room, and rumor has it that her physician at the time was incredibly incompetent could cause anyone to have a seizure I would think.

෴

Antoinette did not know the sex of her new baby for hours after her birth. When Antoinette finally awoke, it was recorded that she said,

> *"Poor little girl, you are not what was desired, but*
> *you are never the less dear to me on that account.*
> *A boy would have become the property of the*
> *state. You shall be mine."*

෴

Little Sophie, the last baby to be born of the marriage was born premature and died at eleven months, and little Louis Joseph, who had also been such a delicate little one for most of his life, died two years after Sophie, when he was seven years old, from tuberculosis. There is no loss more significant in this authors opinion than to lose a child. It is not the normal circle of life as we know it. Losing a child seems to take a part of you with them, and you are never the same as you were before. I am sure this had a profound effect on Antoinette.

❦ IV ❧

MARIE ANTOINETTE
TAKES A LOVER

"You can be assured that I need no one's guidance in anything concerning propriety."

— MARIE ANTOINETTE

❦

Even though it is true in the beginning, Antoinette was not crazy by any means in love with her husband; she did eventually find she had a genuine fondness for Louis. On his part, the King was devoted to her entirely, and he never took a mistress for himself. It showed great restraint on his part which was unheard of with a French King in the 18th century.

❦

Antoinette had several flirtations which were innocent; she

was in love deeply – probably with the implied approval of Louis', pursuant a confidante – to only one man: a Swedish military diplomat by the name of Count Axel Fersen. Some historians want to argue that they were not lovers, but some letters have been found that supply too much information to deny their relationship. It is also thought that two of her children were fathered by Axel.

৩৯৫৩

Hans Axel von Fersen (who was a Swedish soldier) and Antoinette were only teenagers when they first met in 1771 at a masquerade ball held in Paris. She was married but was not yet the Queen of France and Axel's career in the military had just started. He was the same age as Antoinette and was part of the Swedish nobility, but for some reason, he served for Frances Army.

৩৯৫৩

During the masquerade ball, Axel and Antoinette decided to take off their masks and talk to each other. That ball and that talk was the beginning to their friendship that would blossom into far more as time passed.

৩৯৫৩

Antoinette invited Axel to come to Versailles, and it was not long before he was her favorite guest. Every chance Axel had he would travel to Versailles, but it was not long before his career in the military changed and it took him to far off England to live for several years.

৩৯৫৩

After living in England, he was called to the American colonies to fight with the Americans in the Revolution there. It was in 1781, where he served as the aide-de-camp and distinguished himself during the Seige of Yorktown. He was promoted to Colonel because of his bravery in the Seige.

❧

It was June of 1783 when Axel wrote his sister and said he was swearing off marriage. He told her he could not belong to the only person he wanted to belong to, the one who really did love him, and therefore I do not want to belong to anyone else. It was during that summer that he visited Antoinette almost every day.

❧

The king and queen were exact opposites, and some say their marriage was not a happy one. The King liked his solitude, quietness, metalworking and loved to hunt while Antoinette loved fashion, politics, dances and the arts.

❧

During the years that Axel and Antoinette were apart, they sent secret letters to each other. When Axel came back to France from the U.S. Antoinette gave Axel a gift of a small journal. On the journal, Antoinette had embroidered:

"Faith, hope, and love never go to the United States."

in French. Axel had also had made for Antoinette a ring in which was inscribed:

"all leads me to thee."

✦

It was 1784, and Sweden's government again called Axel to Sweden. You will find that most historians on the subject feel that Axel's loyalty stayed with Antoinette and her French monarchy even though he was serving his King Gustav III.

✦

Every time he had a chance, Axel came to see Antoinette and became a more frequent guest all the time. Antoinette even went so far as to give him his own apartment that was above hers.

✦

In October 1787, they were sending each other secret love letters about boring details such as where to place a stove. It was trivial dribble.

✦

Trying to unravel their relationship has for years kept biographers busy guessing, mainly because Axel destroyed the most substantial portions of his journals and one of his great nephews that he left his letters to, censored them and entirely suppressed the rest. In one letter to Axel from Antoinette, she declared,

"I can tell you that I love you."

✦

During 1790, King Gustav III told Axel to go to Versailles as part of Sweden's Corps of Diplomats.

☙❦❧

Axel wrote a letter to his sister, Countess Sophie Piper, in April of 1790 in which he said that:

> *"I am a little happier, for from time to time I am able to see her quite freely in her apartment, and this consoles us slightly for all the unpleasantness she has to put up with."*

☙❦❧

Axel stayed in Paris all of 1791 and through the year he an Antoinette became so much closer, and it is felt by most who followed the history between them that it was at this time that they become lovers.

☙❦❧

But then Antoinette and the entire Royal Family were prisoners at Tuileries, and it gave Axel full and free access to the whole palace.

❧ V ❧

VERSAILLES - A PRIVATE GETAWAY

"I have begun the 'History of England' by Mr. Hume.
It seems to me very interesting, though it is necessary
to recollect that it is a Protestant who has written it."

— MARIE ANTOINETTE

❀

In June of 1774, a few days after Louis XVI gave Antoinette
the hideaway she had told him she wanted. Antoinette
wanted a place that was only for her circle of closest friends.
When Louis XVI gave Antoinette this place, he said to her
'this pleasure house is yours.'

❀

During 1780 Antoinette started spending a tremendous

amount of time at her hideaway, her own private castle on the grounds outside the Palace of Versailles, but she was almost always there without her king.

⚜

Secluded in their luxury hideaway at Versailles, Antoinette and Louis XVI had no idea what was happening with their subjects. They did not know their countrymen had suffered a failed harvest and that the price of grain had skyrocketed and there was rioting in Paris in the streets as the people were demanding that they should be able to buy cheap bread.

⚜

The high taxes were killing them. All the while Antoinette was gambling like crazy, ordering expensive clothes and jewelry and spending money like there was no tomorrow on her private getaway at Versailles, the Petit Trianon.

⚜

It was a three-story neo-classical mansion that had been built on the grounds in Versailles in 1762-68 by Louis XV for his lover. Since Antoinette had a select group of friends that were the only ones invited to go there, it made everyone else jealous, and gossip in the Palace ran rampant.

⚜

They were saying goings-on at the Trianon was perverse and scandalous, which gave anti-monarchist material to spread in their underground cartoons. Just how could the Queen be spending their money, during their time of such financial crisis, all on her secret hideaway.

Antoinette turned a blind eye to all the criticism. She went right on with the remodel by directing architect Richard Mique and the artist Hubert Robert to design a rustic fantasy with artificial streams, caves, and beautiful winding paths.

When Antoinette would have nighttime parties, there would be a Temple of Love Dome with a glass music salon that was lit up by wood fires that had been hidden in trenches dug down in the ground.

In 1784, the creation looked like what appeared to be a village of tumbledown and cracked cottages that were furnished with stoves, billiard tables, and comfortable couches.

There was a working farm on the estate. The total bill for the Petit Trianon was what would be more than $6 million today.

There was in one room a beautiful harp that stood that Antoinette could play and play well enough so that she could accompany Antonio Salieri, a Hapsburg composer and a rival to Mozart that she had invited to visit.

❈

She had mirrored interior shutters, so the queen could lower or raise them at will. Of course, the gossip was that the mirrors were there to surround the beds for all the secret rendezvouses when it was her only intent to keep nosey passersby from looking inside.

❈

Whatever meetings there were, none of them included King Louis XVI, who never spent one night at the Petit Trianon Manor, but he did come by now and then to sit in a rowboat and read to himself.

❧ VI ❧

DIAMONDS WERE NOT
HER BEST FRIEND

"It is true I am rather taken up with dress; but as to feathers, everyone wears them, and it would seem extraordinary if I did not."

— MARIE ANTOINETTE

❦

Antoinette was almost thirty years old, a queen, and the mother of her daughter, Marie Therese Charlotte who was 4 ½ years old, her son, the Dauphin Louis Joseph Xavier, who was almost two at the time in 1785.

❦

She had become a beautiful full-figured woman with brilliant eyes and her demeanor that some interpreted as dignified while others thought she was haughty.

☙❧

About the time of the birth of her second son, Louis Charles came into the world, Antoinette was the victim of one of the most complicated swindles in all of history.

☙❧

Jeanne de Lamotte Valois, a con woman, persuaded one gullible Cardinal de Rohan that she was the Queen's close friend even though Antoinette had never before heard of her.

☙❧

Lamotte had a lover by the name of Retaux de Villette, who forged some letters that supposedly were from the Queen asking the cardinal to purchase a necklace with 647 diamonds that cost 1.5 million francs which in today's money is ($4.7 million). Writing as if she were the queen, de Villette relayed "*she*" was much too embarrassed to ask King Louis XVI for such an expensive present and was hoping the cardinal could purchase it for her. The Queen would reimburse him immediately.

☙❧

After a secret meeting outside in the gardens of the palace with another woman who had been hired by Lamotte to mimic the Queen, Rohan was immediately captivated. When the jewelers brought the necklace to Rohan, he passed it on to Retaux, who had disguised himself as the Queen's footman.

Lamotte's husband then took the necklace and smuggled it on to London so it could be sold off in pieces. In August of that year, the jeweler demanded his payment. Marie Antoinette was furious, and Louis put out the order for Rohan to be arrested.

The trial that followed caused a huge sensation. The Parliament in Paris resisted the command of the king to convict the tricked cardinal and pardoned him.

Lamotte was taken out and whipped, placed a brand on her chest of a '*V*' for voleuse for the word thief and was thrown into prison.

Antoinette who was not on trial, but it seemed that she should have been with the way the people of the country treated her. Universally the people of her country felt she was guilty.

The mess with the diamond necklace just added fuel to the fire for all the scandalmongers and pamphleteering folks who ran with the journalists that were wanting to make the Queen look guilty, corrupt, and greedy.

※

From that day forward, Antoinette could do nothing right. Due to this mess, it made King Louis XVI even more vulnerable. The severe shortage of food, the country was weighed down by taxes, people were so resentful of the Royal Monarchy, and they envied what the United States had for a government.

※

To avoid the nation's ever-nearing bankruptcy, in May 1789, due to the series of wars, King Louis XVI's supporting the American Revolution that weakened England and depleted France's treasury even more, and years of corruption, the King called a meeting of the Estates-General, nobility and commoners, and the assembly of representation of the clergy.

※

As Antoinette's carriage traveled through the streets of Versailles, the gathering crowds that were standing along the way looked on in sullen silence.

※

In the town's Church of St. Louis, in his sermon, the Bishop of Nancy preached against all the outrageous spending of the Queen. The people of the town had dubbed her '***Madame Deficit***' as she was being blamed more and more for the desperate financial straits of the country even though she had already cut back on spending with her personal expenses. But, too little, too late.

❧

Antoinette did not have time to focus on all the gossip about her because she was consumed with worry about her oldest son, who was gravely ill. Before the month was up, the seven-year-old prince was dead of tuberculosis of his spine.

❧ VII ❧

THE FRENCH
REVOLUTION BEGINS

"It is an amazing feature in the French character that they will let themselves be led away so easily by bad counsels and yet return again so quickly. It is certain that as these people have, out of their misery, treated us so well, we are the more bound to work for their happiness."

— MARIE ANTOINETTE

Antoinette, apparently with a better head on her shoulders than Louis XVI, tried to get him to stop the revolt, but Louis XVI, didn't want to make them any madder or start an out and out war, so he said no, and this caused surrendering Paris to the militants.

900 French workers and peasants across the land raided the Bastille prison so they could take the ammunition and arms that were stored there and marking what was to be the beginning of the French Revolution on July 14, 1789.

Later that year, on October 6th, an estimated 10,000 congregated around the Palace at Versailles and were demanding the King and Queen be taken to Paris.

Comte Mirabeau who was leading the anti-monarchist for the National Assembly and had noticed it was the Queen instead of the King that was appearing in court. The Assembly stopped the age-old privileges that pertained to the clergy and all aristocracy in the weeks after the King and Queen had been taken to Paris. The free press declared the changes that had been made, and let the people know that they were Proclaiming the Rights of all Men and they had gotten rid of serfdom.

Antoinette started meeting covertly with Mirabeau about July 1790. By doing so, she was able to win this influential legislator to her side to save the monarchy. By the end of the year, she had started working on an alternate plan to escape from Paris and go to Montmedy which was near the Netherlands that was controlled by Austria.

Then the King and Queen would be able to raise a revolt with the troops that were under the control of Royalist General Francois Bouille. Out of the blue, in April of 1791 Mirabeau died and he had not secured the promise of the Assembly to keep King Louis as a constitutional Monarch. Antoinette and Louis put their plan into action anyway.

But they did not follow Bouille's advice and travel in two light carriages because Antoinette wanted the family to stay together in a large, cumbersome wagon type coach they called a Berlin. It had a silver dinner service, something to press their clothes with, and a little wine chest. Axel had made all the preparations and even mortgaged his estate, so he could pay for the big cumbersome coach.

Late in the day, toward evening on June 20, 1791, the entire Royal family disguised themselves as servants to leave the capital. Axel went with them no further than Bondy which was sixteen miles due east of Tuileries.

The horses were being changed out, and Axel asked Louis to please let him stay with the Royal family to guard them instead of them meeting up again at Montmedy later in two days.

King Louis said no, and many think that it was because he did not want his wife's lover protecting them. Or, that he didn't want others thinking a foreigner had assisted them in fleeing.

❦

October 5th, slightly before noon, several thousand women from the markets that had armed themselves with sickles and spikes, started their march from Paris City Hall walking twelve miles on their way to Versailles. They were protesting the high cost of bread and the fact there were no jobs for the people. They came to take up their stance in front of the Palace.

❦

By the evening of that day, thousands more had joined them, and they were toting guns. King Louis after wavering back and forth as to what he should do, finally thought his family should hide in the Rambouillet chateau. The coachmen brought around the royal carriages, but the angry crowd cut the harnesses, causing their family to be stranded.

❦

At five the next morning which was the 6th of that month, rebels flooded into Antoinette's bedroom and on their way in killed two guards. Antoinette was terrified as she sprang out of her bed and went running into King Louis XVI apartments.

❦

Meanwhile, Louis had gone to Antoinette's room to get her but found she was already gone, so he turned and went back to the dining quarters of his apartment where he found Antoinette and their daughter.

෯෫ඁ

Marquis Lafayette who was commander of Frances National Guard had made it to the scene with more Guard troops and for a short while restored order.

෯෫ඁ

The crowds were still angry outside and wanted King Louis XVI, so they could take him to Paris. Someone out in the group called for Antoinette to come out on the balcony, and she did just that and curtsied. When she did this, a silence came over the mob, and they started shouting, "**Long live the queen!**"

෯෫ඁ

Antoinette had a feeling this reprieve would not last long. When she went back inside, she had a short nervous breakdown. She said,

> *"I know they are going to make us go to Paris, Louis*
> *and I, preceded by the heads of our bodyguards on*
> *the end of spikes."*

෯෫ඁ

She was right; it was only a matter of hours when this very

thing had started; precisely as she had predicted it. They took the Royal family to the capital at the Old Tuileries Palace.

༺✦༻

They didn't lock Antoinette and Louis in, so they could leave the palace if they wanted to do just that, instead they went into their own self-imposed solitude.

༺✦༻

1794 found Louis Charles, still locked up in the Temple Tower, being kept away from his aunt and sister, with his aunt being executed sometime in May 1794. They claimed she was an enemy of their people.

༺✦༻

Eleven months later, in June 1795, Louis Charles who was now ten years old, had not a country, lay down and died in the Tower, more than likely he died from tuberculosis as his older brother.

༺✦༻

It would be six months after his death, that they would return his older 17-year-old sister to Austria for a prisoner exchange. Ultimately, she married her first cousin, who was a Duke. Sadly, she never had children and died at 72 years old in 1851 just outside of Vienna.

❧ VIII ❧

PRISONERS IN
THE TOWER

"No one understands my ills, nor the terror that fills my breast, who does not know the heart of a mother."

— MARIE ANTOINETTE

❦

130 miles due east of Paris, in Varennes, a body of armed peasants attacked King Louis XVI, who they had recognized in prominent Berlin and they forced the Royal family inside a municipal officer's home.

❦

A small group of Royalist soldiers showed up to free them, Louis wavered, because he was afraid he might cause a confrontation with the growing mob outside that were armed. He declined the help of the soldiers and decided to wait for Bouille.

※

If they only had Axel who was a trained officer with them, he would have more than likely taken a more direct approach to the situation and got the family to safety.

※

Agents were sent by the Assembly and had been given the orders to take the Royal family back to Paris. Crowds comprised of mad Parisians were lining the streets as King Louis and Queen Antoinette were escorted back to the Tuileries Palace. They would be held there as prisoners by the countries National Guardsmen. King Louis XVI was ridiculed as if he were a castrated pig, and Antoinette was made to look as if she were an immoral traitor.

※

For the time, the Assembly was going to allow King Louis to stay on as the figurehead for the throne to legalize a new constitution that had been proposed, but he had no actual power politically.

※

At this time Antoinette had been lobbying the moderate Republicans secretly who held seats in the Assembly for the constitutional monarchy, but she was writing to the rulers in Europe that the enormous constitution was nothing more than a "***tissue of absurdities that would not work***" and the

Assembly was a heap of "***beasts, madmen, and blackguards***." King Louis XVI secretly hated the constitution, but on September 14, 1791, he did take the oath to uphold it and to share power with the Legislative Assembly.

❧

Back in Stockholm, Axel had talked the King of Sweden to back him in a new escape attempt. In February 1792, Axel who was branded as an outlaw for his last role in helping the Royal Family escape – snuck into the palace that was guarded so heavily and stayed for 30 hours with Antoinette. It was near the end of this visit that King Louis made his appearance and said they would not take the escape that Axel had planned for them through Normandy. It was around midnight of Axel's second day there that Antoinette told him goodbye for the last time of her life.

❧

King Louis declared France was at war with Austria in April because of the pressure of the Assembly. They knew Austria was going to invade France, so they could restore Alsace (France occupied that at the time) and it would obtain liberty for the Royals.

❧

Suspecting the King and Queen might be working with the enemy, a mob that was armed stormed into the Tuileries August 10th, and they killed more than one thousand noblemen and guards. King Louis XVI and the Royal Familly ran on foot out through one of the courtyards to a nearby

Assembly building. It was there they begged the government representatives to protect them.

❦

What happened was a shock to everyone. The Assembly voted to lock the King, Queen, their only daughter and son, and Elisabeth, the king's sister up in the Temple tower. It was an ominous medieval fortress in the middle of Paris.

❦

September 20th the new National Convention (revolutionary) which was the successor to what before had been known as the Assembly, finally met for its first time. The next day they eradicated the 1,000-year-old Monarchy and then established the new Republic.

❦

The Royal family, or what had been the Royal family were now prisoners being held in the Temple Tower. The following two months were unlike that of any other and were total domestic calm.

❦

King Louis XVI would school Louis Charles, his seven-year-old son, in dramas of Racine and Corneille while the Queen gave to Marie Therese who was thirteen her history lessons, play chess with King Louis, do needlework and sing with the harpsichord.

❦

King Louis's letters he had written to foreign leaders where they were plotting a revolution and counter-attack were discovered in a safe that was hidden at the Tuileries November 20th. King Louis was pulled away from his little family, locked away on the floor below where the rest of the family was and on the day after Christmas they put him on trial.

❀

The trial lasted for three weeks. Those who testified were less than honest about what they swore to tell as the truth. Robespierre claimed at the end of the trial,

> *"It is with regret that I pronounce the fatal truth,*
> *Louis must die, so that the country may live."*

❀

The Convention took a vote, and there were only a few that were '***nae***,' but the vote was mostly unanimous in the fact that they agreed that King Louis had been found guilty in conspiring against the state. Some of the less radical faction felt they should hold the King until the war with Austria was over and then banish him from the country.

❀

Thomas Paine, an English philosopher, begged that the Royal Family be sent to America. It was just not meant to be. They condemned Louis who was 38 years old to die on January 16th, 1793. He could spend only a few hours with his family before going to his final rest January 21st after facing his beheading before a happy crowd of onlookers that was estimated at 20,000.

❦

The State was suffering from an invasion of foreign troops, the Monarchy had been dissolved, and yet, during all of this, the King was sitting calmly eating away at a chicken followed by a peach. He never seemed to lose his appetite even though he wound up in the Temple Prison.

❦

While in his prison cell, he still had three servants at his beck and call, thirteen officers that had domestic duties, and every day he ate four entrees, three roasts, three soups, four desserts, fruits, jams, pastries, and fine wines.

❦

Even the night before he was to be beheaded, while Antoinette was worried to death about him, King Louis still enjoyed a wonderful meal.

❧ IX ❧

KING LOUIS XVI IS
BEHEADED

"I have seen all, I have heard all, I have forgotten all."

— MARIE ANTOINETTE

❧

It seems strange, but even right up till the time for his head to be lopped off, King Louis seemed to be calm and serene. Maybe it was because he had a big full belly and he felt good about the legacy he was leaving behind; well at least it was a type of legacy as far as a culinary heritage could be concerned: '**The Potato**,' which King Louis XVI had vigorously promoted.

❧

The day of the beheading dawned as wet and cold. King

Louis XVI awoke at five o'clock. When the clock struck eight, a troop of guardsmen numbering 1200 on horses showed up to escort the former King on his two-hour ride to the place where he was to be beheaded.

❧

Louis had requested that a priest, Henry Essex Edgeworth, who lived in France, and an Englishman, be with him. The priest recorded the entire event as the King, and he got into the carriage and started off on their journey.

❧

King Louis XVI sat himself down in the carriage, but he was not allowed to speak to anyone, even the priest unless a witness was present, so there was a deep and profound silence. The priest gave the King his prayer book, the only one the priest had with him, and the King seemed happy to get it. The King seemed to become anxious when the Priest pointed out the Psalms that were particularly suited to the situation ahead and the King recited them out loud with the Priest.

❧

The attending officers, keeping their silence, were confounded and astonished at what tranquil Godliness their Monarch was exhibiting, as they had never been near King Louis XVI before.

❧

The long procession kept moving for about two hours; while

along the streets citizens lined both sides, all of them armed, some who had guns, and some with spears, while the carriage stayed surrounded with a body of troops formed out of the most desperate of the desperate people of Paris.

⚜

For an extra precaution, they put before the horse's several drums, so they could drown out any murmur or noise that might be in favor for the King; but how in the world could they have been heard?

⚜

No one showed their faces in their windows or doors, and out in the streets, there was nothing to be seen but citizens that were armed in some fashion. These citizens were all heading toward the commission of the crime, which in reality they hated in their hearts.

⚜

The carriage kept going in silence and then stopped in an ample space around the scaffold: the space was encompassed with a cannon, and beyond that, there stood an armed multitude stretched as far as one could see.

⚜

When the King realized the carriage had stopped, he turned toward the Priest and softly said,

"We are arrived, if I mistake not."

The priest's answer was by silence. A guard stepped forward to open the door to the carriage, and the soldiers would have customarily jumped out, but King Louis stopped them, leaning his arm on the Priest's knee,

> *"Gentlemen, I recommend this good man to you; take*
> *care that after my death no insult be offered to*
> *him – I charge you to prevent it."*

As soon as King Louis had stepped down from the carriage, three guards encompassed him, and they were about to take off his clothes, but he stopped them with pride – took his own clothes off, untied his collar, unbuttoned his shirt, and composed himself.

❦

The guards encircled him once more and would have grabbed his hands, but the King wanted to know what they were doing, and they told him they were going to bind his hands. The King told them to do what you have to do to me but don't restrict my hands.

❦

The footpath that led to the scaffold seemed to be rough and hard to walk on; the King appeared to lean on the Priest. From his slowness with which he walked, the Priest thought that maybe his courage might be failing. When King Louis got to the last step, the King let go of the Priest's arm, and he walked firmly across the entire scaffold; in abject silence. His look alone told you everything, there were fifteen to twenty drums beating but in a thunderous voice the King said:

'I die innocent of all the crimes laid to my charge; I pardon those who have occasioned my death, and I pray to God that the blood you are going to shed may never be visited on France.'

❦

There were a lot of people hollering at the same time to execute the King. They all seemed stimulated, and in seizing with the violence, they dragged the most virtuous of all Kings under the guillotine ax, that with one stroke his head was cut from his body.

❦

It was all over in a second. The youngest of all the guards, probably about eighteen years old, grabbed the King's head and walked around the scaffold so all the people could see what had been accomplished. At first, it seemed like there was total silence; then there were cries of "***Hail to the Republic!***" The screams became louder and louder, and before long every hat was thrown into the air.

❧ X ❧

OFF WITH ANOTHER
HEAD – ANTOINETTE'S

"Courage! I have shown it for years; think you I shall
lose it at the moment when my sufferings are to end?"

— MARIE ANTOINETTE

❧

Antoinette was now being called the '***Widow Capet'***, and six
months later after Louis's beheading, she was moved to a
musty prison that was known as the antechamber for death.

❧

Elisabeth (Louis' sister), Louis Charles, and Marie Therese
were left in the Temple tower. Later in August, Antoinette
saw a familiar face among all her visitors in that of a former
officer, Chevalier Rougeville. While visiting her, he dropped

on purpose at her feet a couple of carnations that contained a note stating he was going to try and rescue her.

⚜

Unfortunately, a guard saw the note, and the public prosecutor Tinville found out that the Royalists were planning on freeing the former Queen (the plan took on the name of Carnation Plot), he decided she would immediately go to trial.

⚜

During the trial, Antoinette was accused of all sorts of falsehoods from incest, genocide to pedophilia. For every charge, Antoinette responded with a cold – indifference- but almost bored reply, except when one of the prosecutors kept pushing her into a corner to give the details about the allegation that she had, in fact, molested her son sexually and that she had also got her sister in law and daughter to go along with it. (Her son had been caught masturbating by a jailer, so he came up with a story to shift the blame to his aunt and mother.)

⚜

Antoinette also had to respond, and she did so with eloquence to the prosecutor's list of accusations – he said she was guilty of making agreements in secret with Prussia and Austria, of sending money abroad to the two younger brothers of Louis' who were in exile and that she conspired with the enemy against France. When she was accused of manipulating the foreign policy of the king, she replied coolly:

*"To advise a course of action and to have it carried
out are very different things."*

৩৯৯

Antoinette stared at the Prosecutor stonily – but he kept
harassing her – he could not figure out why she was not
responding. Why would she not answer him? Finally,
Antoinette stood up and said in a tone that dripped with icy
disgust and pure fury:

> *"If I have not replied, it is because Nature itself
> refuses to respond to such a charge laid against a
> mother. I appeal to all mothers who might be
> present!"*

To the judge's horror, several of the women in the courtroom started applauding the Queen and then there were fish-
wives from Paris that started crying out for this trial to be
quashed.

৩৯৯

There was another pinnacle in the case when the former
Minister of War who had worked for the monarchy, was
brought in to be a witness and was asked to confirm the
Claims of the Republics that Antoinette had been a
supporter of royalist attempting to overthrow the Revolution
by military efforts.

৩৯৯

The old marquis came into the courtroom and bowed to the
Queen, and during his time in the inquisition box he continu-

ously referred to Antoinette as "***Her Majesty***," or "***Your Majesty***" even though the judges' kept insisting he call her either "***the Widow Capet***" or "***Citizeness Capet***."

৩౫৩

It was not a surprise that the Marquis was also sent to the guillotine. It didn't matter with all this drama going on, the trial for Antoinette was just a brief affair that came with a verdict of immediate execution.

৩౫৩

Antoinette was taken back to the prison to wait for her death the next morning. When she passed by other cells where nuns who were in jail for adhering to their Catholic Faith, all reached out through the prison bars trying to touch her garments asking, then begging her to please pray for them once she entered heaven.

৩౫৩

The next morning they came for Antoinette who was no longer the beautiful person she once was, nor was she even pretty. Instead, in every way – even apart from her once unique beauty that was bestowed by real dignity – had turned undeniably and for sure ugly in every definition of the word.

৩౫৩

With everything, she had suffered through during the past four years and the last thirteen months especially had ravaged what was left of her beauty. As Antoinette sat down to write what would be her last letter; her lighting was from two candles in that cold but grim, moldy prison cell in the pre-dawn hours when it was still dark on October 16th, 1793, so if anyone were hoping to be able to see the once beautiful goddess, they would have definitely been disappointed.

◌❊◌

Antoinette's tiny trim waist that had once been encircled in Rose Bertin's designer creations of high fashion had become thickened and coarse. Her beautiful hair that had once been styled in every way from towering cushions with jewels, diamonds, feathers, and powder, down to simple braids that had once been inspired by maidens from the country was now thin, broken and frayed at all lengths.

◌❊◌

It seems that Antoinette suffered from a condition where all the hair on her scalp suddenly turned white. Rumor says that Antoinette's hair turned white the night before her execution with that bloody guillotine.

◌❊◌

We find however in researching that Antoinette's hair took a year to turn grey all over her head and it was even falling out. Her skin that had once been ivory-white was not alabaster anymore, but instead, it was almost ghost like and haggard.

◌❊◌

Her skin was sagging around her neck, chin, eyes, and cheeks that was most noticeable. Her blue eyes that sparkled had clouded and dimmed as she spent weeks and months in that dark prison cell as it had ruined her eyesight. It was regrettably sad for someone so young and beautiful to age this rapidly at thirty-seven years-old in the last four years of her life.

◎❧◉

In the past forty-eight hours, Antoinette had eaten basically nothing. Her body was starting to fall apart rapidly like it knew that her end was near and there was just no point to hold itself together anymore.

◎❧◉

And of all mortifying things to happen, Antoinette's monthly period began just a few days before but had further deteriorated into a horrid, disgusting, nasty, situation of vaginal hemorrhaging. She was constantly changing the menstrual linens she was wearing and doing her best to find a private time to do so modestly.

◎❧◉

She did not want to be interrupted by the guards at an awkward moment, which was difficult. She was a woman who had always protected her privacy and humiliated by any nudity; it was especially embarrassing for her.

◎❧◉

Since Antoinette's husband had been executed, she had been a widow – "***the Widow Capet***," or rather that is what the new government decided they would call her.

❧

She had not seen her only son, Louis-Charles, eight years old now for several weeks, with him being held in a cell below hers, where he was being subjected to horrific physical and mental abuse by his tormentors.

❧

Marie Antoinette could hear him screaming through the floors even though they were made of stone. She would lie down on the floor, sobbing woefully because she was powerless to help her child.

❧

Antoinette after returning from the verdict of the trial was writing the final letter to her sister in law to tell her what was about to happen the next morning.

❧

The following is the contents of the letter:

> *"October 16th, four thirty in the morning.*
> *Sister, I am writing for what will be my last time.*
> > *They have sentenced me to death, but I am not*
> > *shamed by it, because this death is shameful only*
> > *to criminals, so I am going to join your brother.*
> > *Innocent as he was, I hope only to show the*
> > *courage that he showed at last.*
> *I feel calm, and I think it is because my conscience is*
> > *clear, but I am so very grieved for my children. I*
> > *kept existing for them and you, my dear sister.*

You, from the kindness of your heart, have been sacrificing everything to be with us – what a terrible mess I leave you. I do not dare write to my daughter as I am afraid she would never receive my letter. I am not even for sure you will get this letter.

I hope you will be with them again and remind them of the thoughts with which I have never ceased to try to inspire them – mostly, that sound principles and the performance of duties are the prime foundation of life, and that mutual love and confidence will bring them happiness. I trust my daughter will know that at the age she is now she must always be a help to her brother with advice which her experience and affection will allow her to give him; and that my son, in his turn, will give his sister all the care will do her all the services which affection can stimulate; and as brother and sister they will always stay united – that they will take example from us. That even though our misfortunes, how much consolation we have derived from our mutual affection! In happier times, one's enjoyment is doubled when one can share it with a friend – where can one find a more affectionate, a more intimate friend than in one's own family?

I hope that my son will never forget his father's words: Let him never try to avenge our deaths!

I must speak to you now on a matter that is painful. I know how much my boy must have made you suffer. Forgive him, dear sister, remember how young he is, and how easy it is to make a child say whatever one wants, to put words he does not understand into his mouth. I hope a day will

come when he will grasp the full value of your
kindness and of the affection you have shown
both my children.

It remains to entrust you with my last thoughts. I
should have liked to write them before the trial
opened; but, apart from the fact that I was not
allowed to write, things have moved so swiftly
that I really have not had the time.

I die in the Catholic, Apostolic, and Roman religion,
in that of my fathers, that in which I was
brought up, and which I have always professed.
Having no hope of spiritual consolation, not even
knowing whether there are still priests of that
religion in France and feeling that should there be
such I should expose them to great risks were they
to visit me here, I sincerely ask God's forgiveness
for all the faults I have committed since I was
born. I trust that, in His goodness, He will hear
my last prayers, as well as those which I have
long been making that, in His pity and His
goodness, He may receive my soul.

I ask the forgiveness of all those whom I have known,
and, especially of you, my sister, for the sorrow
which, unwittingly, I may have caused you. I
forgive my enemies the evil they have done me. I
here bid farewell to my aunts and my brothers
and sisters. I had friends. The thought of being
separated from them forever and of their distress
is among my greatest regrets in dying. Let them
know, at least, that down to the last they were in
my mind.

Adieu, my good and affectionate sister. I trust that
this letter will reach you. Continue to think of
me. I send you my most heartfelt love, and also to

*my poor, dear children. How heartbreaking it is
to leave them forever! Adieu, adieu. I must now
devote myself entirely to my spiritual duties.
Since all my actions are under restraint, it is
possible that they will bring a priest to me. I
declare, however, that I shall not say a word to
him, and that I shall treat him as an absolute
stranger."*

৩৫৩

The letter stops there, broken off suddenly and is never
resumed. She was right about one thing for sure – the letter
never got to her sister in law. It is said that it was found later
in Robespierre's mattress with a lock of Antoinette's hair.

৩৫৩

Antoinette, not knowing of course, but she was not right
about Elisabeth and Marie as they had not been separated.
They would eventually be separated, but not until they were
going to execute Elisabeth that they followed through with in
May of the next year.

৩৫৩

Why she stopped writing at this point so abruptly, we will
probably never know, as she did not even place a signature at
the bottom of the page. Maybe she wanted some time to pray,
but she knew that whatever priest they sent her would not be
from the Vatican and she would not feel right talking to him.
Another probability is that Antoinette was exhausted physi-
cally and mentally and needed to lie down.

Thirty minutes later, the last of Antoinette's servants – had entered her cell hesitantly, where she found her stretched out, lying on her bed, staring up toward the ceiling with her eyes wide open.

Seventeen-year-old Rosalie had tears running down her cheeks as she approached her Queen's bed. Rosalie had made some soup for Antoinette and begged her to please eat it. Marie Antoinette seeing how distressed Rosalie was, tried to eat a few spoonfuls before getting changed.

The sun had come up over the city, and you could hear the drums beating that was announcing the death of Marie Antoinette. Soldiers were taking their places all through the town, to prevent any attempts there might be to try and rescue the Queen while she was being taken to her beheading.

In the prison cell, Antoinette realized she had to change her menstrual linens once again – the cloths were soaked with blood. The guards in her cell would not leave when she asked them to give her just a few minutes to change her underwear. Embarrassingly, she did not have any choice but to kneel in one of the corners while Rosalie tried to shield her from prying eyes, so she could change her linens.

It was then time for Rosalie to help Antoinette to get out of her widow's dress which she had worn since her husband had been beheaded. The new Committee decided she could not wear her mourning clothes to her death. Another dress was brought in for her to wear, but Antoinette managed to put some black ribbon on her bonnet, to show respect for her late husband.

Into her room came the Public Executioner, Sanson to cut off the last of what was left of her hair to make sure her neck was exposed to the blade of the guillotine. Her displeasure was evident when they bound her hands behind her back, and they roughly led her from her prison cell, where they left Rosalie, hysterically sobbing and one little golden watch which been given to her as a gift from her mother when she was a child. That watch would lay there ticking and counting away the last minutes of its owner's life.

Once in history, in centuries gone by, the prison had actually been a Palace, so as odd as it sounds, it was appropriate that it was Marie-Antoinette's last residence on this earth.

Antoinette was then forced out in the courtyard, she was handled roughly and placed in the back of an open, wood card that had been used to transport prostitutes and criminals. Her husband had been allowed to ride in a carriage that was closed and was allowed to choose his priest. They wanted to parade Antoinette's shame in front of all of Paris, and of course, a Republican priest was placed next to her. He attempted to offer his spiritual services, but, as she had promised to her sister in law, she refused them politely.

⚜

Stupidly and curiously, the new Republic did not allow her to wear black meaning that Antoinette was to go to death wearing what at that time in history was considered a strong color – white.

⚜

It was what was referred to as '***chick glamour***' like Anne Boleyn got to wear with a dark gown or Mary the Queen of Scots who got to wear a crimson dress. By most accounts, you will find that when Antoinette's ghostly white figure was walked through the double row of navy blue dressed soldiers that lined her pathway. The entire crowd responded with leaden, stunned silence. Past them a woman rode who was not crowned in feathers; not covered in jewels, not outlandishly dressed; a woman that appeared so bereaved that even her mourning dress had been removed from her; a woman whose clothes that were left in prison were going to be sent back to the women prisoners after Antoinette's death.

⚜

Before she even got to the guillotine, her being and body had been deleted – by leaving her in only white. By erasing her, it revealed more than it ever concealed, by condensing it down to the entirety of her dangerously fashionably past.

She was placed in white, the color of a young bride's skin tone. White which is the color of the whalebone used in a corset stay. White the color used for costume parties and snow. White the color of real powdered hair. White the color of the Boehmer's necklace of diamonds and that of "***Austrian***" feathers of the ostrich. White the color of the true-blue emblems for the loyalist. White the color of the locks of hair that Antoinette saw her executioner slipped into his pocket when he sheared her hair off her head before she would meet her fate. White the color of holy heaven, martyrdom, and of eternal life. White the color of a ghost that is too willful or too beautiful to die. White the color of the pages where Marie Antoinette's story will be written over and over and over.

❧

When Antoinette moved by the thousands of onlookers, she heard some call out their insults; some would laugh, some would spit towards her while others pointed; a few cried out,

"Hail to the Republic!"

Others in the crowd stayed silent; the secret service saw many royalists in the onlookers, with the grief-stricken faces that were very conspicuous. A working-class woman held up her baby boy, to prove her show of motherly solidarity with the Queen. The Queen sat on the carriage as if she did not see any of it – her face remained frozen in an appearance of dignified acceptance to her fate. You could see no fear on her as she rode closer and closer to her death.

There was only one point when Antoinette's eyes filled with tears and lips started to quiver, and that was when they passed the Tuileries Palace because it was here that she and her little family had been together under house arrest four years ago.

As the cart passed by the Rue St.-Honore, a great revolutionary artist by the name of Jean-Jacques David had made a fast sketch of Antoinette. He had sketched her more heroically vicious, making her look proud, bloated, disdainful, and pure ugly. By looking at this picture, no one can deny the dignity that Antoinette had to endure with shame on her drive to her place of execution. What a revolutionary artist may have seen as ugly disdain, others see as heroic dignity. Looking back in time makes it much better to give an opinion on any issue than to look forward and try to predict the future.

It would be an hour later when the cart would reach its destination, where the guillotine stood in front of a large statue of '**Lady Liberty**' as she would be renamed, once her image was re-invented and remodeled, and then sent to the United States the next century.

Antoinette quietly stepped down from the rough carriage and

looked up at the guillotine. The priest thinking that he would make himself helpful said,

> *"This is the moment, Madame, to arm yourself with courage."*

With her death being imminent, Antoinette thawed for a second and turned toward the priest and replied with a smile:

> *"The moment when my ills are going to end is not a moment when courage will fail me."*

❧

Antoinette walked up the steps with confidence; she stopped to apologize to her executioner when she thought she had stepped on his foot. Having her hands tied behind her back had limited her sense of balance and caused her to have issues with her freedom of movement.

❧

They strapped her into place, lowered her beneath the blade and secured her. Sanson walked around her, hit the lever and down went the blade. At 12:15 p.m. on Wednesday, October 16th, 1793 Marie Antoinette of Austria and Queen of France was dead, just two weeks before turning thirty-eight years old.

❧

Her dead body was put in a coffin and dumped into a mass grave behind the Church of the Madeline. In 1815 King Louis XVIII returned to the throne after the exile of Napoleon, and King Louis XVIII ordered the bodies of his brother, Louis XVI, and Marie Antoinette to be disinterred and gave them a decent burial next to other French Royals inside the Basilica Cathedral of St. Denis where they lay in rest to this day. He also had placed stone statues that looked like the royal couple that appears as if to kneel in prayer that sits above the underground vault.

❦ XI ❧

ANTOINETTE WAS SO MUCH MORE

"No harm will come to me. The Assembly is prepared to treat us leniently."

— MARIE ANTOINETTE

❀

Many think that Antoinette was famous for the quote,

"Let them eat cake."

It is said that when she heard her people were hungry and did not even have any bread to eat was presumably what caused the beginning of the French Revolution.

❀

There seems to be no hard evidence she is the one who uttered those words and many feel that it was not in her character to have said anything near that; even though she led a lavish type lifestyle, she was one who gave to charities and did have compassion for the standard class of her countrymen. Most feel the comment came from a Marie-Therese, who was a Spanish princess that married King Louis XIV.

❧

Even people who felt that Marie-Antoinette was an airhead and a spendthrift had nice things to say about her. Some of which were:

> "She was never evil or cruel. She never betrayed France, and at moments of great danger she showed a kind of generosity."
> "Mine is not grief...No; it is all admiration and enthusiasm! She was, for King Louis XVI, "an unparalleled Princess."

❧

Maxime de la Rocheterie, who wrote:

> "She was not a guilty woman, neither was she a saint; she was an upright, charming woman, a little frivolous, somewhat impulsive, but always pure; she was a queen, at times ardent in her fancies for her favorites and thoughtless in her policy, but proud and full of energy; a thorough woman in her winsome ways and tenderness of heart..."

Marie-Antoinette died a heroine and a lady. One does not have to be a monarchist to see that. The worst criticism that can be fairly levied against her is that, as a young woman, she was "*a little frivolous, somewhat impulsive.*"

❧

Antoinette would have been happy to have just been the ceremonial queen rather than the role she was forced to play, but due to Louis' and his many weaknesses it pushed her into taking on more of his roles than she wanted and the people of France could not find forgiveness for her for that fact.

❧

The sketched cartoons that showed her trampling their constitution. She was given complete blame for the bankruptcy of their country when there were plenty other in the extreme-spending, lavish court that bore equal liability.

❧

None of it mattered, they condemned her for being Louis' wife and made her a symbol of tyranny. Antoinette was only a scapegoat for everything that went wrong in France's dynastic system according to new absolutist theory. Since Louis and Antoinette refused to compromise in any way, they lost everything.

❧

Thomas Jefferson, who was the minister to France at the time stated that if Marie Antoinette could have been placed in a convent, the French Revolution would have never taken place. This author thinks that Jefferson mouthed too much.

❦

Antoinette being the last Queen of France was defamed as the essence of all the evils of the monarchy. At this same time, Marie Antoinette was also raised on a pinnacle of beauty and fashion, with compulsive knowledge on her own choices in jewelry and clothes in her wardrobe along with the endless speculation regarding her extramarital love life.

❦

It takes both of these to judge Antoinette's character flaws; some as prevalent in our times today as it was in Antoinette's lifetime. It would depict how her life and her death was symbolic on the downfall of the European Monarchies. The last queen of France has been slandered as the personification of the evils of the royalty.

❦

At the same time, Marie Antoinette had also been exalted as an extremity of fashion and beauty, with obsessive knowledge of her choices in wardrobe and jewelry and endless speculation about her extramarital love life. Both of these take on Marie Antoinette's character and show the tendency, as common today as it was in her own time, to portray her life and death as symbolic of the downfall of European monarchies during the time of a revolution that seemed to cover the globe.

❦

By now, I am sure you must be wondering what happened to Antoinette's lover Axel. He had become an adviser that was trusted by the King of Sweden. He couldn't forgive himself for not saving Antoinette, the only woman he loved, when they took a flight to Varennes.

❦

He asked himself many times,

> *"Why of why did I not die for her on the 20th*
> *of June?"*

as it wrote it in his journal. June 20th, 1810, nineteen years later, there was a mob from Stockholm, who wrongly believed he had poisoned the heir to their Swedish throne, and they beat Axel to death with stones and sticks.

❧ XII ☙

CONCLUSION

❧❧❧

As was said earlier in this book, it is always easier to look back on one's life and see the mistakes one has made. Some, we wish we could do over as we would have done things differently. But life is not to be lived in that way. It is not to be lived where we know what is ahead of us as well.

❧❧❧

Poor Antoinette never had a chance, to begin with, because she was forced into the marriage and was expected to rise to the occasion. So much was required of her as a Queen because her husband did not seem to be interested in his duties as the King of France.

❧❧❧

Louis XVI was only interested in the fun part of being a King, and it seems he was very interested in eating. He had several hobbies that held his interest, and I feel he truly respected his wife, but one gets the idea he only loved her like a sister, not as a wife should be loved even after his surgery. If he had truly loved her as he should have, and he could have satisfied her in the beginning, I doubt she would have taken on a lover.

❧❧

If she had had the attention of Louis XVI, I doubt that she would have spent the money she did, but she was so bored with life.

❧❧

It seemed the justice system of France lacked a lot, and someone somewhere was blade happy with the guillotine. How wrong can that be?

❧❧

It does not matter; the bottom line is this... Antoinette nor Louis neither one deserved to be imprisoned or beheaded as they were falsely accused with '***trumped up***' charges to give the people someone to blame for the problems of their country and the blood should be on their hands. I hope God had mercy on their souls when they died and had to meet their maker.

STRENGTHS

- During her marriage ceremony to King Louis XVI there was a stampede during the fireworks show that killed 132 people; for twelve months Antoinette and her King gave of their private money for spending to the victims and families of the victims. (Always help those in need even if you are not rich, you are always richer than someone else, even if you feel poor.)
- Antionette taught her daughter to help the peasant children in their country and to give up her own Christmas presents so that blankets and fuel could be purchased for the poverty-stricken, and they took food to the ill. (Teaching your children, nieces, nephews how to be benevolent to others and forgo a gift for themselves that will only give them momentary pleasure is a valuable lesson that will stay with them for a lifetime.)
- It is reported that Antoinette opened a home for unwed mothers. (Assisting others in such a plight and having no place to start is that of a servant's

heart. Do what you can for others at any opportunity you see.)

- At her farm on Trianon, she built cottages for several peasant families to live there and work for her. (She provided homes for several peasant families without making them feel like they were charity cases by having them work on the farm on Trianon letting them preserve their dignity.)
- Most people never knew of the good works of Antoinette as they were too busy focusing on her negative points.

WEAKNESSES

- She had issues with her spending habits. She spent money she did not have on jewels, clothes and her hideaway mansion.
- She spent too much money on gambling.
- She was a social butterfly in some ways but preferred to isolate herself from the subjects of the country to be surrounded only by people she enjoyed.
- The people of France felt one of her weaknesses was the fact that she was from Austria, who France was forever at odds.

❧ XIII ❧
MORE GOOD READS ON MARIE ANTOINETTE

❦

- Who was Marie Antoinette? By Dana Meachen Rau
- Marie Antoinette: The Journey by Antonia Fraser
- A Day with Marie Antoinette by Helene Delalex

YOUR FREE EBOOK!

As a way of saying thank you for reading our book, we're offering you a free copy of the below eBook.

Happy Reading!

Printed in Great Britain
by Amazon

23196902R00057